D0195611

THE GOLDEN ROAD

RACHEL HADAS

THE
GOLDEN ROAD

Poems

TRIQUARTERLY BOOKS
NORTHWESTERN UNIVERSITY PRESS
EVANSTON, ILLINOIS

TriQuarterly Books
Northwestern University Press
www.nupress.northwestern.edu

Copyright © 2012 by Rachel Hadas. Published 2012 by TriQuarterly Books/Northwestern
University Press. All rights reserved.

Printed in the United States of America

10   9   8   7   6   5   4   3   2   1

Library of Congress Cataloging-in-Publication Data
Hadas, Rachel.
    The golden road : poems / Rachel Hadas.
       p. cm.
    ISBN 978-0-8101-2859-0 (pbk. : alk. paper)
    1. Grief—Poetry. I. Title.
PS3558.A3116G65 2012
811.54—dc23

                                          2012015841

♾ The paper used in this publication meets the minimum requirements of the American
National Standard for Information Sciences—Permanence of Paper for Printed Library Materials,
ANSI Z39.48-1992.

In memory of George Edwards (1943–2011)

and

for our son Jonathan

The gold road curves.
The living pass the dead.

CONTENTS

Acknowledgments   *ix*

I

The Pattern   *5*
Plutarch on the Plane   *6*
On the Ferry   *7*
Nostos   *8*
First Persons   *10*
Generic   *11*
Complete Poussiniana   *12*
Cranes   *13*
No Good Deed   *14*
The Long Way Home   *17*
The Cloak   *18*
Amphora   *19*
The Dream Retriever   *20*

II

The Study   *23*
Rear Window   *24*
Body of Book   *26*
Help   *27*
The Language of Women   *28*
Woman and Girl   *30*
In Memoriam, Rachel Wetzsteon   *31*
The Last Glimpse   *33*
The Address Book   *35*
Etymology   *36*

III

The Onset   *39*

The Fortune-Teller   *40*

Between Brattleboro and Bellows Falls   *42*

Valentine's Day   *43*

Only So Much   *44*

Boston Naming Test   *46*

Neurology Floor   *47*

Spring Sunday in the Park   *48*

The Question   *49*

Carl Schurz Park   *50*

Winding Stair, Lost Sneaker, Rising Tide   *51*

The Book in the Bag   *52*

Macbeth   *54*

Double Bed   *56*

New Year   *57*

Moons   *58*

IV

Driving Back with My Son   *61*

Host at Last   *62*

Joe's Pond   *64*

The Swing   *65*

Ballade on Pumpkin Hill   *67*

The Hammock   *72*

The Tall Wet Grass   *73*

After the End of Summer   *76*

Storing the Season   *77*

Honey   *78*

The Golden Road   *80*

Acknowledgments

Able Muse: "The Last Glimpse"

American Scholar: "The Study"

Common Review: "The Long Way Home," "Rear Window," and "The Tall Wet Grass"

Evansville Review: "Amphora"

Examined Life: "The Onset"

First Things: "Complete Poussiniana"

Hudson Review: "The Address Book," "The Language of Women," and "Woman and Girl"

Literary Imagination: "Double Bed," "In Memoriam, Rachel Wetzsteon," "The Pattern," and "Spring Sunday in the Park"

Measure: "Ballade on Pumpkin Hill"

New Criterion: "First Persons," "Plutarch on the Plane," "The Swing," and "Valentine's Day"

New England Review: "The Fortune-Teller" and *Macbeth*

New Republic: "The Golden Road"

New Yorker: "New Year" and "Only So Much"

Progressive: "Host at Last"

Raintown Review: "Winding Stair, Lost Sneaker, Rising Tide"

Slate: "Body of Book" and "Generic"

Times Literary Supplement: "Between Brattleboro and Bellows Falls" and "Nostos"

Upstreet: "The Dream Retriever" and "Joe's Pond"

Yale Review: "No Good Deed" and "On the Ferry"

THE GOLDEN ROAD

THE PATTERN

On the train to the airport a little white dog peeps
from the tote bag in a woman's lap.
Once you see the pattern, it recurs:
origin, journey, wound, and destination,
journey originating with the wound,
destination cycling back to journey.
Band-Aid, crutches, cast, that little dog:
wound we carry with us tenderly
journeying toward a cure. The destination
doubles as origin. A tall cupped candle
shines through two red hands. Interior threshold.
Journey. Crystal column. Origin.
Bath of silence where you wash your wound.

PLUTARCH ON THE PLANE

I'm almost sure I hear
before we leave the ground
the man in the seat ahead of mine
enunciate the name
"Plutarch" on his cell phone.
Perhaps a classicist?
Possibly a professor
at the university
in the city we
are flying toward this January noon.
Maybe he knew my brother,
who taught here. Maybe he
studied in his youth
with my Plutarch-loving father.
Nothing would be more likely.
The world shrinks steadily,
or time, turned palpable,
pulls people toward each other.
As we file down the aisle,
I could easily speak to him.
Feebly or discreetly
or for some other reason,
I let the moment go,
and we get off the plane.

ON THE FERRY

The voyage is the easy part. Between
departure and arrival, here I sit
baking on the deck, and cogitate
        all I have seen

        sailing along alone,
saluting light and water through the long bright day
        that arcs between the two.
Samos: the mountain, when the sun goes down,

quenches the same radiance I knew
        some thirty years ago—
now no less radiant, I ascertain;
which having done,

I pack my bag and sail away alone.
        Another port at dawn
        and out next day by noon,
old narratives unfinished, new begun,

cut off midconversation: call me soon!
        Not yet. The sea paths shine
and beckon, fade, and vanish into foam.
        I sail alone.

NOSTOS

The village broils in the long noon.
Over the pool the swallows skim.
To the west the massive stone
mountain broods and bides its time.

I am Odysseus who returns,
I am Penelope who waits,
the midday sun that burns and burns,
Telemachus who hesitates.

So many seasons come and gone.
Recognition flickers: do
I feel sure of this face, that name?
Penelope, who never knew

for certain whether it was he—
wavering, a mirage of heat—
has taken on new life for me,
who find I also hesitate,

later remembering a face
or voice I think I used to know.
How much, eyes shut, could I retrace?
Here was the bakery years ago.

This was the skinny boy who ran,
a fisherman's son, along the quay,
now a lean and grizzled man
who looks at me and quizzically

asks, "Are you Rachel?" I agree;
guilty as charged. But years have blurred
our mutual identity.
It's me—but "me" is just a word.

Thirty-some years. A generation.
Over the pool the swallows skim.
As leaves fall, so it is with men.
The great stone mountain bides its time.

FIRST PERSONS

All those youthful outpourings featuring "we":
To whom was I speaking?
Was "we" no more than a gesture
Intending to demonstrate
That I came coupled,
That therefore I was desirable
And no sad solitary?
For whom was I speaking?
There must be other things to be than we.
And yet as one gets older
The "I" fades too.
Even as the shadows of experience lengthen,
One's core seems less substantial.
Those youthful poems that did not say "we"
Spoke as "I" instead. But who is she?
I am not a forest nymph, a tree,
A sibyl or a goddess or a bird.
I am leaning toward transparency.
I hope to end as echo of a word.

GENERIC

The little boy who snuggles next to me
while I read him *Millions of Cats*
and we meow together
"No, I am the prettiest!" "I am!" "I am!"
is five. I'm sixty. The book is eighty-one.
I have read it before.

Durable, evocative, stale, weary;
renewable, exhaustible, and placid;
benign or neutral, shifty as the moon;
obedient to undeciphered laws:
what we take for granted
vanishes, reconfigures, disappears.

Samos, Squirrel Island, Spetses,
Cherry Tree Walk down by the Hudson River:
the massive stones on which I love to perch
and gaze into the changed, unchanging water
don't tell me their age, and I don't ask.
I have been here before.

COMPLETE POUSSINIANA

Deep in myth, these galleries keep their counsel
but redistribute all the elements.

Nymph rides goat, attended by a satyr
who pats her rump to help her keep her seat;

putto rides goat, attended by a nymph.
Two other satyrs from behind a bush

leer at a nymph reclining in a grot.
By a Maenadic, irrepressibly

chortling nurse-attendant, infant Bacchus
is given wine to drink. And over here

Eurydice sees the viper, lifts her skirt,
scurries—in vain, we know, but she does not.

This story isn't over yet. Behind them
all, a massive hilltop fortress built

of solid stone is somehow catching fire.
Perspective, possibilities peel back:

reluctantly we leave one world, reenter
another, where we have already seen

stone burning and a crane collapsing. Now
get ready for the season of the snake.

CRANES

A few springs ago, several enormous cranes
toppled over, smashing into buildings,
killing their operators, also others
going about their daily business. Now
when we see a crane looming in the sky,
we edge away
and cross to the other side of the street.
It's not only the danger;
that immense suspendedness is eerie.

The stillness in the skyline
(permits pending so construction halts)
puts me in mind of Dido,
too crazed with love to remember to rule her city.
The young men in her army forgot how to drill.
And motionless as if paralyzed,
or swaying all but imperceptibly
over half-finished buildings,
gigantic cranes hung idle in the sky.

No Good Deed

No good deed goes unpunished,
my mother often said.
Though what about the not-so-good
deeds we forget we did?

Or what about the prizes
life offers and we take,
confident as we pocket them
there has been no mistake?

Add to this that the wicked
flourish like the green bay.
No bad deed's unrewarded,
we also ought to say.

No good deed goes unpunished
is one of my sister's laws.
But through each person's private air
there floats a cloud of flaws.

We're wounding and neglectful,
sluggish and cruel. Unused,
our gifts come back to haunt us
like creatures we've abused.

Might this explain the nasty
results of random acts
of kindness? Let me tell you one
that stopped me in my tracks.

On Ninety-Eighth and Broadway,
one day this rainy June,
a well-meaning young woman
tried to help a blind man

(I knew him by sight—my sight—
and thought of him as Pew)
over a puddle at the curb.
A kindly thing to do?

He thrust her off, not gently.
He shouted at the air,
his face a mask of fury,
There's always a puddle there!

Never touch a stranger!
His raised voice pulled me back.
Others turned too. She stood there
motionless, mouth slack,

incredulous her gesture
had met this more than rough
response. And it gets worse. As if
his vileness weren't enough,

add to it my silence.
I saw the ugly scene
chilling her warm intention
yet failed to intervene,

reproach him or console her.
Troubled, I slunk home.
I turned my back, I failed to speak.
I only wrote this poem.

Anger wields a whiplash.
Cut one of us; all bleed.
Tamely, I let him savage her
For doing a good deed.

Never touch a stranger!
The blind man's crazy logic
fits right in with *No good deed*'s
apotropaic magic.

Help him over a puddle.
Go on, be a good neighbor.
Conceivably you'll enter
some kingdom with this labor.

But it is just as likely
that the very man
you reached out to so simply,
my Good Samaritan,

will shake his fist at you. Don't take it
personally; read
it as the vicious boomerang
released by a good deed.

THE LONG WAY HOME

How far around we seemed to have to go
to reach the lost familiar. How wide
and deep the detour, over mountain crags
quaking with thunder, or through tossing seas

toward an island drowsing in disguise.
A story at once ancient and brand-new:
fresh as a headline, every morning's tale
trumps yesterday's. Combine these elements:

the grown child lost and weeping,
longing to leave home, longing to come back;
the mother and the son beside the sea;
the father and the daughter on the mountain.

The final act. A storm is rolling in,
and flames creep up the mountain gorge, where he
kisses his daughter one last time; departs.
How far we had to come to see that kiss!

So you and I leave passion's theater,
homeward bound by local or express,
images tucked beneath our coats for warmth,
sheltered from winter's cold like loneliness.

THE CLOAK

Quisque suos patimur manes

They might be any happy couple
except I happen to know them.
How do I know they're happy?
He's chuckling, turning toward her
as they hurry north on windy Broadway.
From under her fur hat she smiles at him.

Spell, curse, or blessing, the by-now familiar
law operates: I see them,
they do not see me.
Color of bruise and shadow,
the cloak of invisibility
settles over my shoulders.

The afterlife turns out to be not quite
an afterlife. I am alive; I live there.
I step over the threshold
into a penumbral zone. I move
from solitude into a ghostly precinct,
a place of dimness, of transparency.

I'm stepping out the door of the Garden of Eden
as they stride past. Obedient to the law,
they do not see me. They are carrying
bags of provisions back to the apartment
they will unlock, go in, put down their bundles,
take off their coats, and shut the door behind them.

AMPHORA

Every jug, as Epictetus tells us,
has two handles. This amphora, though,
fished up from the dream-depths of the Mediterranean,
    I carry by one handle,
    balance it at my waist.
I do not know what it contains; I know
    I must not drop it.

Boulders crop up along a jagged path.
    Fresh water flowing
    downhill makes slippery going.
    Accordingly I plant each foot
    deliberately
    and as if it were a baby
hug the precious burden to my hip.

THE DREAM RETRIEVER

The red-bearded young traveler in shorts
carrying a backpack stood ahead of me
in a slow line at the bank this morning. Not
until he stepped up to the teller's window
did I see that he was barefoot. Whereupon
my own feet, as if they were naked too,
sensed the bank's chilly and synthetic floor
with an urgency I didn't understand

till I remembered that in a dawn dream
I had been running, running in my sock feet,
desperate, through endless corridors
in search of what—my shoes? No, something vital
and bigger I had lost. We each, it seems,
can rescue some unguessed-at stranger's dreams.

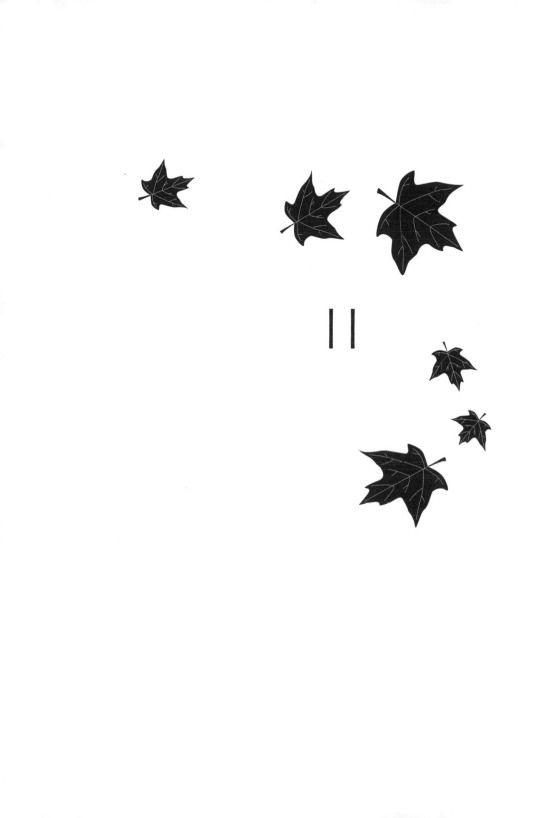

THE STUDY

Map in a frame and fire in the grate.
Dust sheets soberly drape the furniture.
The challenge is to sit down in a chair.
Stripes on the rug. All straight lines. Nothing bends.
On a side table, a square tray with tea;
a fat book (Bible? dictionary?); pens.
Which of these is the portal? Which the key?
The hard thing is to wait.

Who entered this room's realm,
walked up to the table, and sat down?
What person do we seek and sometimes find
momentarily, then lose again?
From what unseen
window does light slant in?

REAR WINDOW

As Philip Roth has said somewhere,
writers are best viewed from the rear.
The curious interlocutor
is forced in this way to infer

the writer's doing nothing else but stare
at typewriter, computer, pen and paper,
since all that is discernible (Roth said)
is the back of the writer's head.

No more than Orpheus must he or she
turn around. What would there be to say—
"Eurydice, Eurydice"? No, no;
the beloved companion is long gone,

and Orpheus must wend his widowed way
through Hades's pale, stale throngs.
How can he sing his songs?
In order to transform his pain

to melody, he needs to be alone.
Even were she somehow to reappear,
he would (I know musicians) beg her
to keep a careful distance, please be still

if only for a while:
"Honey, let me compose this monody!"
She sighs. Her thoughts sway like a grove of trees,
women's voices rustling in their leaves.

For her, part of the loneliness of hell
was having no one near at hand to tell.
For him, her reappearance lets him be
absorbed and silent with impunity.

He sweeps the strings and tries out a new mode.
She takes a pen and tests it on the white
medium of stillness where they meet.
The mutual space is crucial. Emily

Brontë's self-portrait in her diary
shows her writing, notebook on her knee.
All we can do is peer at what may be in there.
As Roth would like, the sitter's turned her back.

BODY OF BOOK

This is one way to talk about a book:
I woke into the locus of my body.
In sleep's thick envelope, what poems fit?
Dream-card sealed with a kiss and then sent out.
What we meant was musing, nothing else.
Did the dream not spring from memory?
Remembering who said what or what I read:
the sin of middle age, misattribution.
Cherished, it writes itself upon your skin.
I could tell the time of day without looking at the sun.
Salted with a tear and wiped and sent:
you take it with you to the land of sleep,
body of book to read and to be read to,
out into the world, its face still damp.

Cherished, it writes itself upon your skin.
You take it with you to the land of sleep.
Remembering who said what, or what I read,
I could tell the time of day without looking at the sun.
Body of book: to read and to be read to,
salted with a tear and wiped and sent
(the sin of middle age, misattribution)
out into the world, its face still damp,
dream-card sealed with a kiss and then sent out
until we all went wearily to bed.
I woke into the locus of my body
where what we meant was kindness, nothing else.
Did the dream not spring from memory?
This is one way to talk about a book.

HELP

Caught in the dream of a book,
who doesn't look up startled when the spell is broken?
I need help to trace the raveled thread
leading to conversations with the dead.
Gesturing with some urgency, my father,
leaning closer than he did in life,
is still far off. I ask him all the same,
"What do I do now? You have been there. Help me!"
Peering down the distances between us,
he offers no advice, but waves a hand
toward a wall of books I cannot read.

THE LANGUAGE OF WOMEN

Here is a letter from a stranger. When
I open it, it unfurls like a fan,
flashing before me stages of her long
life in dizzying succession.

Motherhood, widowhood, mountaineering, cancer;
horseback riding, teaching, poetry;
remarriage. A postscript: "You needn't answer."
A gust of heated air blows out at me,

chatty, confessional, and intimate.
And yet I know that once I put it down,
not ready to be answering it yet,
the letter will fold back into a fan.

A letter from a friend arrived as well
today—no vita, but a catalog
of decisions made for good or ill;
and husband, mother, children, cat, and dog.

Both letters scintillated with detail
without succumbing to the weight of fact.
Each item was set down with the same skill
that keeps a dancer poised before her act.

What women say, or write when they're apart,
pours forth with so much fluency and grace
the boundaries that separate each heart
become almost impossible to trace.

Neither of these writers seemed intent
on immortality through apt quotations.
The mildest impulse toward prose ornament
was thwarted by their strenuous vocations:

steering their households through the choppy sea
of the domestic, they had little leisure
(even though this was 1993)
or inclination for style as pleasure.

Whitecaps, dancer, folded fans—I know it,
a cauldron of mixed metaphor indeed.
But women's lives are fissured, and to show it
a multitasking tongue is what we need,

not limited to the dialect we speak
among ourselves. Men listening at the door
complain we sound like chickens: *cluck cluck cluck
gabble gabble* with contempt or fear

or maybe envy that we women know
at least two modes of speech and maybe three:
the public and the private, high and low.
Diglossic without being binary,

we're fluent too in what our mothers taught
if we were lucky: it is possible
to think, laugh, love, and rage with mouth tight shut,
a secret language open to us all.

WOMAN AND GIRL

A slight young woman in a long dark coat
walking toward me at twilight on One Hundredth Street
is clasping in both arms a big bouquet.

She drops its wrapping in the garbage can,
not even breaking stride to do this; then
holds up the now nude blossoms, breathes them in.

A little girl clutching her father's hand
(finger, rather) as they cross Broadway
looks up gleefully at clouds, squeals, "Rain!"

Naked flowers burying one face,
the other tilted back to drink in sky.

In Memoriam, Rachel Wetzsteon (1967–2009)

She disappeared in the dead of winter.

Before you went into the dark,
you wrote about Sakura Park,
small Rachel. Railed enclosure, plaque . . .
Oh, what can bring our dear dead back?
Or do they ever leave at all?
My son speaks of a dad-shaped hole.
Father, daughter, mother, son:
where can we say that ends begin?
Summer 1966:
My father and I gaze over the Styx—
I mean the Hudson—near that same place,
that park. Our last talk face-to-face;
I did not see my father again.
He died next month. I was seventeen.
Long absent, yet a presence too,
still now, in everything I do.
He died. The next year you were born.
In a lovely poem you envision
a Greenwich Village encounter with Auden,
besneakered bard six decades older
than toddler Rachel in her stroller.
He would have read your work with pride,
I think. When your own father died,
you lived, you wrote, you laughed, you cried.
True to your lineage a city lover,
you went for runs down by the river,
reminding yourself in "The Long Run,"
"I have a body." That was then.

You're in our neighborhood no longer.
Life and death, Rachel: which is stronger?
Where did you go that we can't follow?
The realm of Hades, not Apollo.
I see it as a sooty black
cave, a narrow cul-de-sac.
But your lonely stifling tomb
is also—see?—an anteroom.
Beyond the smoke, the choking heat
wait other poets whom you greet.
Auden, Larkin, other friends—
hard to see where the circle ends
of kinsmen holding out their hands.
Love, so treacherous while you lived,
shaped those elements that survive:
infectious laughter laced with pain,
the poise and wit in every line
love set in motion. Your Muse burned bright
till your own hands put out her light.
May you who left in the dead of winter
safely cross the cleansing river.

THE LAST GLIMPSE

RW, 1967–2009

The dead, below or on the other side,
although they bypass lighted rooms
and skirt the conversations of the living,
lately have begun

to turn up—sometimes in the street, sometimes
climbing the subway stairs—as passing figures
that loom abruptly into familiarity.
Sometimes we seem to see them

not palely present, not peripheral,
but face-to-face. *Red hair, those eyes like lamps;*
that height, that hat, black pants, even that laugh —
I see, I hear her: instant, piecemeal, gone.

The last time I glimpsed her among the living,
she was standing on the corner
of Broadway and a Hundred and Tenth Street,
not, as I first thought, talking on a cell phone,

not talking to anyone at all,
rather intently watching
through the November twilight
either shoppers bustling in and out

of the West Side Market
or else the brightly lit
fruits and vegetables on display
or something inward that I couldn't see.

Alert, observant, listening, alone . . .
I saw her from a bus. We rumbled on.
But was this the last time, or did I dream it?
Were there other last times? Were there none?

She who stood close to the fruits of autumn
before they were taken in
as protection from the winter cold
at the turn of the year herself went underground.

The trees are bare still, Rachel, two months on.
The days are getting longer. When you died
in late December, each day was already
adding on a sliver of new light.

THE ADDRESS BOOK

When it came to the deaths of friends,
my mother's practice was to x
out their names in her address book. I
draw one diagonal slash, as if the name,
address, phone numbers all were a mistake;
then in the lower right, an afterthought
or postscript or correction: one last date.

The book whose pages I am turning now
offers no such stark delineations
of before and after, lived and died.
Each day lifts up a fresh face all the cleaner
for having forgotten its own name.
Hours, weeks, months, years roll mildly on.
The end's the same.

ETYMOLOGY

The Greek word *hero* is cognate with *hour*
(*hore*), also meaning time or season.
The etymology has a stark reason:
he sprouts like a young tree or a spring flower

and is cut down. O creature of a day!
A sunny morning followed by noon rain:
petals scatter over the wet lawn,
autumn prefigured in the end of May.

III

THE ONSET

When did your illness start? I and our son
reckon it must have happened in between
the time you held him throned
on your shoulders high above the world
and when the towers fell. Between the time
you reasoned with him in the talking chair
and his freshman year. Between the time
you and I used to swing him as he walked
(one-two-three whoosh! he held a hand of each)
and when he started sleeping with his girlfriend.

Such lavish spans, dwarfing mere puberty,
leave years to play with. I could narrow them,
approximate with more precision when
the shadow started ever so slowly creeping over you.
But clarity is not available
as in remembered endings: the last time
we talked or laughed; no, the last time we looked
each other in the eye and saw a future.

THE FORTUNE-TELLER

When I impulsively had my fortune told,
I was too cheap to spring
for a crystal ball or lines across my hand.
Cards did the trick. Who knew
why this woman drifting up Broadway
had happened to catch the fortune-teller's eye?

The gypsy might have understood; not I.
Too few, too many secrets to be told.
Trees in leaf along Broadway
dappled and canopied the street with spring
reflections green inside her crystal: new
data inserted by an invisible hand.

Particles swirl and clear: time lends a hand,
and seasons, sleep, the weather of the eye.
"You love someone," the gypsy said. She knew
the arrow: was she waiting to be told
the target? As mercurial as spring,
a muffled weight, an ache that floats away

leaving in its wake a veil Broadway
gleams through: two young lovers hand in hand
glisten like the crystal globe of spring
too brilliant this May evening for me
to gaze into. Do I need to be told
news of desire? How could I not know

the future I broke stride to peer at? No—
I didn't, though. In her own sphinxlike way
the gypsy saw I wanted to be told

not whom one day I might take by the hand
or look intoxicated in the eye
or stroll with down the green arcade of spring,

but something else. "You love?" No answer sprang
to my lips. It was getting late, I knew.
Glanced at my watch; then her (in her dark eyes
swirled possibilities but no one way)
and put five dollars in her outstretched hand
and went away without having been told

a future I had not sought to be told,
cupping the green spring evening in my hand,
cherishing, trying to say yes, not no.

Between Brattleboro and Bellows Falls

Darkness rose as day behind the trees
Dwindled, although the occasional metal roof,
Mimicking a river or a lake,

Might briefly lob back light
Until the train sped on
And the specious glow was lost.

We move past trees
And then an open field, then trees again,
And day when we emerge

Is that much closer to ending:
Light has gone down a notch.
Change works like that.

The pace of decline seems vanishingly slow,
But look up: the sky's darker. Gazing blankly
Into the twilit window, I snare a fragment

Of conversation floating back from when
We still had conversations,
Or I thought we did. But the next day

It was for you as if that conversation
Had never happened. I looked up
And saw the sky had changed.

VALENTINE'S DAY

Frigid, but the days are getting longer.
They fly by like the pages
of a calendar in an old movie—
a likeness to a likeness.

Going outside, you brace yourself for cold.
But by the time you're used to it enough
to stand up straight, unclasp your arms,
raise your head and face into the wind,

you face another weather. So with this:
I drank your diagnosis, took it in.
There is no other way to move but onward.
Not that winter's over yet; and not

that spring is imminent. But change is constant.
What is there to prepare for?
Soon I'll stop bundling up in layers of wool
each time I venture out.

Only So Much

I bend to the open notebook; distracted, turn my head.
Tiny brown ants are climbing up a stalk of goldenrod.

It isn't clear what goal they hope to reach.
I pick up a sharpened pencil, start to sketch.

A passing cloud; the sky goes dull. I shut
the notebook and open it from the back, to write.

There is only so much we can notice all at once.
Now this morning's dream makes an appearance:

packed lecture hall where students overflow
to aisles and floor. What do they want to know?

I have the sense they're gathered here to learn
some kind of surgery. The brain donation

card, wallet-size, arrived in this morning's mail.
I close the notebook. The patient ants still crawl.

A sudden breeze: the grasses toss their tops.
Wild strawberry runners are clambering over this rock,

where, if I sat here long enough, eventually
the tough, lithe tendrils would also crisscross me.

I could climb down from my temporary tower,
go to the house and fill a glass with water,

get out my watercolors, dip my brush,
memorialize this moment with a wash

of color; sketch the runners, trace a border,
as if imitation equaled order.

Or I could take a walk down to the brook
or stretch out in the hammock with a book

or let my thoughts' red runners trace a line
to the null magnet of my husband's brain,

the hospital where he's "undergoing observation,"
the arid wide plateau of the condition—

a battleground to which I will return.
But there is room for only so much attention.

BOSTON NAMING TEST

Pages of images: a child's blunt scissors;
escalator; pretzel; tennis racket;
igloo; camel; wreath. Scooped out of syntax,
each object's still the entrance to a world
of story and association.
But this is not a game. These words are clad
in the uniform of their profession.
They are employed by the Boston Naming Test,
apparently so called because they prove
almost impossible for you to name
as, neither for the first time nor the last,
I sit beside you, helpfully not helping.
You stand up, push your chair back from the table,
and walk away before you've finished failing.
It's been a long morning, says the doctor,
shuffling the pages with their orphaned icons
into a folder. He abandons us
together in a silence one might liken
to a sheet of paper either blank
or scribbled over with an alphabet
nobody can read,
or else to a calm sea
closing over your head.

NEUROLOGY FLOOR

The same sea, says Elizabeth Bishop.
Over and over the same, the same.
I disagree, says Heraclitus.
You can't step into it again

(he means the river). Both are right,
and both are wrong. I do remember
the Hudson: broad, unwrinkled, blue
in the cold sunlight of December.

If you have changed, then what of me,
river? I'm aging, unlike you.
You were here first, you'll be here last.
You go with—no, you are the flow.

You pour yourself into the sea.
The harbor mouth is out of sight
from this eighth-floor window's view
as afternoon turns into night.

Bridge, park, river, sky, and sea,
always changing, seem the same,
allowing for the season's shifts,
as we wade deeper into time.

I and my husband, close together,
stand at the window, watch the river.
A gull wheels toward the Palisades.
Sunset is ambered in forever.

SPRING SUNDAY IN THE PARK

Squinters from winter on parade
stroll through springtime's promenade:
a froth of blossoms, living lace,
the annual bursting out again.
Commit this vernal filigree
to memory: shadows; sun on skin.

Walking through a bower of blossom,
courting couples in each corner,
or in an ark where every other
creature turns, avid, to its mate,
opens its mouth and starts to speak,
I am a solo passenger.

Lover murmurs to eager lover,
mother to child and child to mother,
playmate to playmate, sister, brother,
the homeless man crouched in a corner,
alert and hungry, seeking eye
contact with each passerby:

faces light up with comprehension,
and I am stabbed by deprivation.

THE QUESTION

One way I know he knows who I am:
he roams around after I've left the room,
looking for me. Or that is what they say;
I really only know what I can see.
Sometimes he smiles at me.
He nods when I ask, "Do you remember?"
He opens his mouth as if to speak.
I hand him grapes. He takes them
delicately, between finger and thumb.

The question isn't whether
he recognizes me but whether I
recognize him. There isn't any answer.
Sometimes we sit by the river
and watch the seasons. Spring turns into summer.
Fall turns into winter.

CARL SCHURZ PARK

The crosstown bus, river to river,
takes me from one world to the other.
Fall in the park: a Halloween
costume contest for dogs. In spring
a moving frieze of bicyclists,
skateboarders, dog walkers, lovers,
many parents pushing strollers.
Sometimes—oftener now—a few
passersby steal a glance at you,
tall, slack-jawed, holding my hand,
striding swiftly. We reach the river.
Look, a boat! I'd like to linger:
you've turned away already, pacing
restlessly from now to then.
We pause to buy a popsicle
from childhood's Good Humor Man.

WINDING STAIR, LOST SNEAKER, RISING TIDE

Scurrying down the winding stairs to the corner,
I found myself in a familiar place,
greeting neighbors, knowing every face,
but also waist deep in cloudy water,

and struck by something I'd forgotten, ran
back up the stairs to put my sneakers on,
then squelched back down,
only to realize one shoe wasn't mine,

so flapped back up, the warm and brackish flood
lapping and swirling, to give back the shoe
(whose was it, though? I knew, or thought I knew),
then back down to the complicated world,

treading water, with my chin above
the rising tide, and paddling to wherever
I had to go, and struggling to remember
what first had plunged me in this maelstrom: love?

The Book in the Bag

May '92, Waverly Place.
My friend Charlie lay in bed.
I looked at his beautiful blind face
and took a book from my bag and read

Emma. Austen sets the scene
in Chapter One. He smiled: "I see.
Highbury opens like a fan."
I leaned over. We kissed good-bye.

Fast-forward. Slush replaces green.
Ten years have passed, or maybe more.
Tethered to a slow machine,
I'm giving platelets at Citicorp,

leafing, with the hand that's free,
through Keats's letters. "Trouble and pain
school the soul, do you not see?"
Then out into the world again.

2009. It's Christmastime.
I am seventeen years older
than that spring evening. What new tome
is tucked in the bag slung over my shoulder?

Orlando Furioso! Full
of maidens, knights, a magic steed . . .
My husband, captive in his cell
of silence, can no longer read.

In the ER we share a chair;
no room to extricate the book.
The Hippogryph zooms from the sorcerer's lair;
I do not even need to look.

I unbutton his coat. No need for speech.
The weapons that I need to fight
this battle are within my reach.
I settle in for a long night.

MACBETH

This spring I took myself twice to *Macbeth*.
The point was not the plot,
although its onward arc in fact occasioned
with a weird and unexpected beauty
more than one relish of resemblance
to what I had been going home to every night.

The play unfolds largely at night,
yet my days too had a savor of *Macbeth:*
firstlings of heart and hand; the family resemblance
of "I have done the deed"; the headlong plot
no sooner hatched than executed; spooky beauty
of rooky wood and owl's cry mapped onto my own occasion.

I too had had occasion
to do a deed, then lie awake at night
when darkness only offset some lost beauty;
had had what I thought of as my Lady Macbeth
moment. Though I told myself my plot
really bore not the least resemblance

to Mac and Lady M's, resemblances
pressed in like revenants. "How all occasions
do inform against me," from a different plot's
complexities complains a pallid night-
owl of a hero younger than Macbeth
and far more conscious of his haggard beauty

in a world whose tense sardonic beauty
wags its finger. Some resemblances
to the world stalked through by the Macbeths

presented, of all things, an occasion
for laughter. "'Twas a rough night,"
acknowledges the murderer in midplot,

thus adding to my husband's ongoing plot
an unexpected hiccup. Call it beauty.
"Last night was a rough night,"
emailed the social worker. Resemblances
let tragedy yoke disparate occasions
even with the perilous stuff *Macbeth* is made of.

Plot (Aristotle knew this) is a storehouse of resemblances,
beauty of imitations, occasioned
by our rough nights, the rough night of *Macbeth*.

Double Bed

Lying near the edge of the double bed,
my zigzag should fit snugly
into the curves and hollows of another body.
But I have nothing to wrap myself around
or brace myself against
except two disembodiments: memory—
evocative but taking up no space—
and the jagged humps of argument,
ethereal yet resistant. When I sleep,
I angle myself around a dialectic;
I catnap curled up around the new
configuration. Not new, but not old.
For since you have been vanishing
so gradually for so many years,
new is becoming shabby, worn, familiar,
a present, no beginning and no end.

NEW YEAR

Blue January light, cold, scoured, clear.
From the Sandia foothills looking down
and back to where I came from, and the town
spread out below, then back to the past year,

or three or more years carrying this load,
how do I feel unburdened: free and light?
Unanchored, dizzy, my precarious tight-
rope lowered to a mere terrestrial road?

The blank new month requires divination.
Sword, wand, ship, sandal: at the Flying Star
(we talk our way along; improvisation),
the cards laid out spell struggle, choice, and pain;
also a white horse champing in a green
meadow, a maiden moving down a long dark stair.

MOONS

Around a mirror frame in the concert hall,
decorative moons move through their cycle.
Change isn't so schematic, as a rule.

There is no clear-cut destination.
Each fresh attempt's another iteration.
Every solution's an approximation.

When I asked about a timetable,
the doctor said, "I don't have a crystal ball,"
and then proceeded to give an estimation.

There's no arrival. There is a gradation.
We wait awhile, or longer than awhile,
then step into a further vestibule.

Why should the sequence ever end at all?
If I crane my neck, I see a sickle
moon already fattening to full.

IV

DRIVING BACK WITH MY SON

One way to picture it: a west to east
trajectory, straight horizontal line,
time ticked off as tidily as space.
From this linearity there float
bubbles of otherness. Ethereal,
exempt from map or calendar or clock,
too fragile to hold on to, they englobe
pasts we leave behind us as we drive,
simply by moving as we move, through space,
simply by living as we live, in time.

Yet aren't we also steering
back toward a pair of childhoods,
his and mine? For here we are again,
tethered to place and weather, rain and sun,
Caledonia County, early June.
Softly, as evening blots out afternoon,
in the sky the bubbles fall and rise.
Random as fireflies,
they float and spin and wink and disappear.

HOST AT LAST

If I am host at last,
It is of little more than my own past.
—James Merrill, "A Tenancy"

Summer: time to visit the old house.
Nostalgia is a kind of quenchless thirst.
Mooning over marks the years have made,
I used to pine for all that had been lost.
But nothing's ever thoroughly erased.

Sandwiched between the future and the past,
generations dreaming in each bed
toss (who's alive?) and turn (and who is dead?),
brush past the present as a passing guest
spends one night, then wakes and takes the road.

Faint ancestral echoes barely guessed:
what was it our predecessors said?
Shake out the musty sheets. Wipe off the dust:
tasks of a mother or an aging host
sandwiched between the living and the dead.

I used to pine for all that had been lost.
Mooning over marks the years have made,
shake out the musty sheets. Wipe off the dust.
But nothing's ever thoroughly erased.
Tasks of a mother or an aging host:

brush past the present as a passing guest
tosses and turns, then wakes and takes the road.

Nostalgia is a quenchless kind of thirst.
What was it our predecessors said?
Summer. Time to visit the old house.

JOE'S POND

In a tepid, weedy, murky pond
the amber of iced tea,
we went swimming after lunch. Ten strokes
out from the muddy little strip of beach
brought me to a zone of gliding quiet
and fresh perspective. Cottages
previously seen only from the road
looked from the water bigger, more complex,
also more vulnerable, open to the gaze
of any passing swimmer who might choose
to peer at lives in progress from the rear.
On one unexpected second-story porch
facing the water, an American
flag was flying. Near the flagpole's base
a white dog lay so still
I thought it was the statue of a dog
until it rose to its feet and shook itself
and walked away toward an invisible inner room.

THE SWING

The Bowens are at home, but they don't hear me.
Across the yard their massive barn waits, empty.

A square of shadow: the great open door.
I step inside. The swing's still hanging there;

and in the drizzly, drowsy afternoon
this cloudy August Sunday I sit down,

push off, am launched out toward the soaking green,
then back, then forward: lawn to barn to lawn.

Five decades' distillation, like a dream:
nights in the loft; Paul walking on that beam;

the mounds of ripe manure and moldy hay,
the swing how many children till today

swung and still swing on . . . Two bright windows frame
Ralph and Sue, who both look much the same

as when half a century ago I saw
them first. He's rocking, reading, back to me,

lamplight glancing off his snowy hair;
she's talking on the phone in a blue chair,

both fixed on other times and places, drawn
separately away from the routine

where, waist-deep, neck-deep, both of them are wading
along a track the years keep on eroding,

just as on my own parallel path I
move forward, sink down simultaneously.

BALLADE ON PUMPKIN HILL

What is this rustling I hear
Through the plywood-thin partitions?
Mice and squirrels are everywhere,
But this is the ghost of generations'
Worth of family conversations—
Faces, voices I should know.
That was another summer, though.

Two or three, gathered anywhere,
Talk about their absent cousins.
Jim Quimby's defective new wood floor
Rotted—but my mother's patience
Held, and someone patched the portion
No one had—somehow—fallen through.
That was another summer, though.

Debbie buys fudge at the Danville fair:
One quarter pound, a measly portion.
The aging house requires repair,
Eliciting vague admonitions
From waves of visiting relations.
We wave good-bye and watch them go.
That was another summer, though.

An old piano beached upstairs
Plays host to years of composition.
At splintery tables, in shiny chairs,
Writers scribble their creations.
Judges judge sundry competitions.
August is fast; July is slow.
That was another summer, though.

Boys on the porch till three or four
Deep in the realm of mage and dragon;
Rachel in hammock, bed, or chair,
Rereading Dickens and Jane Austen;
George pondering a chess position:
Capture in memory, then let go.
That was another summer, though.

Here every ailment has its cure.
For poison ivy, jewelweed potion;
For insomnia, fresh air,
Plenty of food, and mild exertion—
This soporific accumulation
Loosens tensions; they let go.
That was another summer, though.

Like a full moon, tranquil and rare,
Dreams here shed cool illumination
On the terrain of the past year:
Regrets and fears and motivations;
Even, with luck, an indication
What puzzled sleepers next should do.
That was another summer, though.

Clues are hidden everywhere.
Bats proceed by echolocation;
In this house we prefer to steer
More as if by divination.
Open a book: triangulation
Points you toward readers long ago.
That was another summer, though.

Teachers use summers to prepare
Or simply read for recreation.
My late half brother's desk Shakespeare
With many a marginal annotation

Offers up distilled perceptions
Penciled in fifty years ago.
That was another summer, though.

I and my father, strolling here
Later than any calculation
Can foretell in his career,
Enjoy a ritual conversation
About chipmunk generations.
Each season's new one he calls Joe.
That was another summer, though.

An avid gardener, my mother
Tended toward spells of green abstraction.
George gives the compost heap a stir
With similar preoccupation.
Lacking such patience, such passion,
I note a blossoming golden glow.
That was another summer, though.

Tempting to see as metaphor
The annual planting of the garden
And growth and harvest every year,
Good smells rising from the kitchen,
And a contented shared digestion.
Each day's a season, said Thoreau.
That was another summer, though.

In August, if the night is clear,
We lie and watch the constellations
Sparkle, until a meteor,
Slicing its dignified position,
Contrives a fleeting new relation
Among the stars with its cloudy glow.
That was another summer, though.

Decades do cause wear and tear.
My mother dies; next the foundation
Begins to slope and shift . . . From there,
It doesn't take much imagination
To picture utter ruination—
Bare ruined choirs where cold winds blow.
That was another summer, though.

Vulnerable to northern air,
Largely lacking in insulation,
Furnishings secondhand and spare—
The house still signifies vacation,
Breathes out a sly beatification
It's weirdly able to bestow.
That was another summer, though.

The damp and drowsy atmosphere
Lends itself to lamentations,
Though for just what is never clear.
The steady, stealthy march of seasons?
Human reluctance or impatience?
I want to stay. I have to go.
That was another summer, though.

My memory stretches fifty years.
How can I not feel trepidation
Speaking of people who appear
Only in terms of vague summation?
Would ghosts endorse this peroration?
I'll never ask; I'll never know.
That was another summer, though.

"I marvel at the ferocious power
With which bad family relations
Repeat themselves, and what is more,

Good ones suffer attenuation
From generation to generation,"
A colleague writes me, full of woe.
That was another summer, though.

I'm not so sure we should despair.
Although of self-congratulation
I superstitiously beware,
Today I'm brimful of emotion—
Naturally mixed, but a large portion
Feels like joy. Love and let go?
That was another summer, though.

THE HAMMOCK

Or maybe heaven. A peeling away; a process
rocking rhythmically toward abstraction;
sheer veil through which meaning tried to glimmer
but kept on changing. Was it infinite?
Was there no
nub, no summery sliver, crescent moon?
Creak creak, says the hammock. Less is more.

THE TALL WET GRASS

i

A memory my sister just unearthed
of the first rainy summer in this house:
she ventured out into the tall wet grass,
wondering what we were doing in this place.

Fast-forward half a century. People come
and go; the house endures. Nature moves on.
The trees my father planted, towering, shade
and dwarf the lawn. "This is a pastoral poem

you're writing," said my nephew. The swing set
where he and his sister played,
the early gardens that my mother made—
such yesteryears leave barely any trace.

I am the housekeeper who keeps the house
and all our heads above the tall wet grass.

ii

"Is it worth it, all this stewardship?"
I asked my niece. "Go write a poem," she
replied. A good idea:
the medium of ambivalence being verse

and I the mistress of the might-have-been,
the maybe or if only or what if,
a territory poems flourish in.

I tended poems here while I was not
weeding the garden. When my mother died
the flowers languished. Here my husband wrote
music while he could; here he can still
stir the compost heap. "Eep" was one

of the first words that our son spoke,
who's coming with his girlfriend in a week.

iii

To enter this damp kingdom annually
is to dip into an Edenic pond,
lost world of childhood, innocent and free,
quick pang of joy plunged into and splashed out of
as we towel off to face the world's dead weight—
weariness, obligation, and grief.

"This is the poem I hope you'll write," said C.
Both our husbands suffer from the same
insidious dissolution of the brain.
Both now are sixty-five, near speechless. Then
after such ragged respite from the real,
a day's, a week's unknown and dewy green,
flowers poking through the tall wet grass,
to turn back to our other lives again.

iv

I lost the thread, I dropped a stitch, my thought
slid sideways. Logic, as so often, lapsed.
How did we get again
from tall wet grass to Eden?

It was no distance. It was barely one
step. The merest shift was needed
in perspective for the patient house
to become a place of refuge.

People in the golden age complained
how yellow everything
looked. And in this emerald oasis
what do I complain of? Yesterday
all day the rain drummed down. No hint of sun.
And yet my eyes were dazzled by the green.

After the End of Summer

Vegetables glowing in the garden,
walks in starlight, or the smell of wood smoke:
enough time evidently had to pass
before all these sank firmly into place.
Not that they had exactly
vanished or been forgotten,
but that they gained in clarity with distance,

so that the brown brook when I finally sat
and listened to it spoke a single word
over and over in its water voice,
a voice born out of silence
different from uneasy human silence,
that cloudy curtain filtering out sound,
or aching hollow longing to be filled.

STORING THE SEASON

The problem is the prodigality:
blackberries, apples in profusion, each
by its respective nature hard to reach.
Tangle of brambles, berries glossy black:
even to graze them with a fingertip,
you have to stretch.
Then rosy apples clustered on a branch
too high to touch—
the problem is too much.
Go for what you can eat:
berry a bucketful, boil into jam;
slice apples, cook, and strain into warm sauce.
Inhale the rising steam,
fragrant distillation of this late

summer, which offers other treasures too,
but less digestible. For what to do
with misty mornings burning off to blue?
With spangled webs that delicately lace
two blades of grass? You can't consume a place.
How to assimilate that lichened rock
on which I like to sit
and dream and gaze at lines of drying hay
striping the field? Can I take these away,
pack them and then unpack, arrange them, spread
them out like Christmas presents on a bed?
If gifts, for whom? For everyone. And why?
The rending gold of August ending—I
can only fold it into poetry.

HONEY

*The actor Richard Burton could not remain in a room
with a jar of honey, even if it was concealed in a drawer.*
—Allen Shawn, *Wish I Could Be There*

Honey poured into a mason jar
and hidden in a drawer has no odor,
yet somehow, thick and dumb,
signals its brimming presence to the wary.

Who will break the seal and spill the sweetness?
Stumbling in the kitchen, no radar
to lead us to the jackpot, can we sense
the golden treasure under lock and key?

Or do I mean a golden treasury?
The bees of the invisible, their honey
distilled and strained, placid, immaculate—
no fragrance, no vibration, and no sound.

Virgin as oval tawny pendant tear
At beehive-edge when ripened combs o'erflow . . .
the wall is loosening, honeybees.
Landscapes we discover as we go:

I see a kitchen table, appetites
sociably swarming. Plates. My thoughts are all
a case of knives. Lips licked.
Crunch of buttered toast. A sticky savor.

Chairs scrape, curtains blow.
Out to the sunny lawn, lilacs in bloom.

The bees build in the crevices of loosened masonry;
I heard the bees from there growl in a hum.

So, Goldilocks, upstairs and to your room.
You're sleeping in my bed now with my bees.
Whose helmet now will make a hive for bees,
Oh golden child the world will kill and eat?

With thanks to R. M. Rilke, Robert Browning, W. B. Yeats,
George Herbert, Erica Dawson, George Peele, and Sylvia Plath.

The Golden Road

On a September road I met my son
walking the other way. I had the hill
to climb; he was returning from a run.
    No surprises; he
    knew I was nearby,
as I knew he was. But precisely where
our paths might meet was a benign surprise.

The road was rutted, plastered with gold leaf.
Did our eyes, as we neared each other, meet?
More of a full-body recognition:
    this tall young stranger
    striding silently
around a bend, who paused on seeing me
(however I appeared) and then passed on.

Autumnal radiance thickened
by complications, memory, history—
nothing startling, in my mother's phrase.
    The gold road curves.
    The living pass the dead.
Old and young acknowledge one another;
then each takes their separate path ahead.

Oh Muse, peel off your dove-gray cardigan.
September, fallen leaves, and cool noon sun:
I rounded a gold curve and saw my son.